# Praise for
# The Invisible Toolbox

"Kim Jocelyn Dickson has given us a gift. In lively and loving language, she opens The Invisible Toolbox and shows us what's inside: opportunities for connection, inspiration, imagination, conversation, and joyful play. Literacy encompasses so much more than the important ability to read. Parents, teachers, and all who love children will be inspired by the author's passionate advocacy, and helpful, compassionate instruction."

—*Amy Dickinson, "Ask Amy" advice columnist, NPR's "Wait, Wait...Don't Tell Me!" panelist, bestselling author*

"The mark of a great teacher is not just enabling a child to do well in class, but also in giving that child the instruments she needs to succeed and love the subject forever. I wish everyone could have Ms. Dickson as their child's teacher as I did, but *The Invisible Toolbox* is the next best thing!"

—*Dr. Richard Chang, pediatrician*

"*The Invisible Toolbox* shares a simple truth that rises above the hectic commotion and flood of information parents are subjected to: 'Reading aloud to your child from birth is one of the greatest gifts a parent can give.' This book will tell you why this is so and what you can do to develop a lifelong love of books and reading in your child."

*—Jeff Conyers, president of The Dollywood Foundation and Dolly Parton's Imagination Library*

"As a pediatrician who sees firsthand the struggles and tears of the children who have empty Invisible Toolboxes, I am thrilled that Ms. Dickson has written this book to show families how to avoid all that heartache. I wholeheartedly recommend that all parents read this book!"

*—Kathryn Lin, MD*

# THE
# INVISIBLE
# TOOLBOX

## ALSO BY THE AUTHOR

*Gifts from the Spirit: Reflections on
the Diaries and Letters of Anne Morrow Lindbergh*

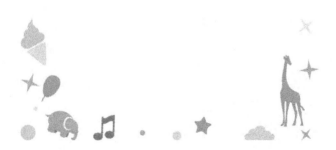

# THE
# INVISIBLE
# TOOLBOX

## THE POWER OF READING TO YOUR CHILD
## FROM BIRTH TO ADOLESCENCE

What Every Parent Needs to Know to Prepare Their Child
for Kindergarten and to Instill a Lifelong Love for Learning

## KIM JOCELYN DICKSON, MA

TURNER
PUBLISHING COMPANY

Turner Publishing
4507 Charlotte Avenue • Suite 100 • Nashville, Tennessee 37209
www.turnerpublishing.com

Cover Design: Jayoung Hong
Cover illustration: Jayoung Hong / Shutterstock @GraphicsRF
Author Photo: Mike Coeyman
Layout & Design: Jayoung Hong

The Invisible Toolbox: The Power of Reading to Your Child
from Birth to Adolescence

Library of Congress Cataloging-in-Publication number: 2019954716
ISBN: (p) 978-1-64250-203-9 (e) 978-1-64250-204-6
BISAC category code FAM034000, FAMILY & RELATIONSHIPS /
Parenting / General

Printed in the United States of America

# Table of Contents

**Chapter One**

    The Secret of the Invisible Toolbox: A Loving Letter

    from Your Child's Future Teacher ............................................................. **10**

**Chapter Two**

    Build It with Love: How Reading, Singing, and Speaking

    to Our Babies Form the Structure of Their Invisible Toolbox ........... **18**

**Chapter Three**

    Kindergarten and the Invisible Toolbox:

    Discovering the Tools Inside .................................................................... **26**

**Chapter Four**

    The Greatest Gift of the Invisible Toolbox, or,

    Why We *Really* Read:

    Awakening the Inner Life of Your Child ............................................... **48**

**Chapter Five**

    The Parent's Toolbox: How You Can Become Your Child's

    First Reading Teacher, Get Past Your Own Hurdles,

    and Enjoy the Treasures Inside ............................................................... **54**

**Chapter Six**

    How to Read Aloud to Your Child: From Birth to Adolescence ..... **66**

**Chapter Seven**

    Important Do's and Don'ts ....................................................................... **84**

Recommended Resources ................................................ 106

Recommended Reading Lists Per Age Group ................... 108

Recommended Websites and Organizations .................. 116

Acknowledgments ..................................................... 119

About the Author ...................................................... 120

Endnotes ................................................................. 121

# Chapter One

# The Secret of the Invisible Toolbox

## A Loving Letter
## from Your Child's Future Teacher

---

Dear New Parent:

Congratulations! Your precious little one is here. There is no feeling in the world more wonderful than holding your tiny newborn for the first time. Your heart expands with warmth and love and protection in a way you never could have imagined until now. As you begin a journey with this miraculous new life you have created that will take both of you far into the future, into places known and unknown, you will do everything in your power to ensure your baby's path is as full of hope and promise as it can be.

As well-meaning parents, we all want our children to thrive. Regular pediatrician visits, vaccinations, sleep routines, proper nutrition, feeding, bathing, cuddling—we do all of these things because we want what is best for them. But there is one more thing that is essential, and it's one that is as important to our growing child as all the things we do to take care of our baby's physical needs. This necessary thing is one that you may already know—or perhaps may have forgotten or haven't fully understood.

As someone who has been in your shoes as a parent *and* taught children just like yours in elementary school for decades, I'd like to share with you what I've learned about this essential thing over the years.

Flash forward five years, and imagine with me what your child will look like on their first day of kindergarten. At this moment that day may seem a long way off, but believe me, it will be here before you know it. Can you see your child in the brand-new school clothes that you've bought for this special day, down to the sneakers with laces so white because they too have never been worn? Under a fresh haircut, there may be a big grin or perhaps a look of apprehension. Your child knows it's a big day, just as you do. On their back is a crisp new backpack, and in one hand a lunchbox filled with favorite things. All of this equipment is recently acquired, full of promise and expectation for the future—and probably decorated with a favorite superhero or three. Who will that be, you wonder? The picture is almost, but not quite, complete. There is more. And here is the secret.

In your little one's other hand, they carry something else. It's a toolbox, but it's invisible. Unseen though it is, it will be carried to school on the first day of kindergarten and every day after that, all through your child's academic career. Whether or not it contains the most essential tools will have an enormous impact on those years and far into the future.

Every child who comes to school carries this Invisible Toolbox. Some children arrive with their Toolboxes brimming with all the tools they need to be successful. They are the fortunate ones. Some children, however, arrive with Toolboxes that are empty. For them, school will be a struggle.

So what is this mysterious Invisible Toolbox all about? It's very simple. Children who are read to regularly by their parents from very early on arrive at school on day one with Toolboxes overflowing with the essential skills they need to be successful students. Because here is the simple truth: *Reading aloud to your child from birth on is one of the greatest gifts a parent can give.*

I've taught grades one through five for nearly thirty years and began to understand the Invisible Toolbox during a long stint teaching third grade in a public school in California. Valley Oak was a wonderful public school, the kind of place people move into a neighborhood for just so they can send their children there. I often called it a "private school in a public-school body" because its teachers were so dedicated, creative, and hard-working, and the amazing principal knew each of the over eight hundred children by name. The children felt known and cared for at Valley Oak, and most of them experienced success and thrived. Still, there were some who did not, despite the fact that they too had entered a robust kindergarten program taught by outstanding and experienced teachers and had equally strong teachers and curriculum through the primary years. These students entered third grade still struggling with reading and, consequently, other subjects. *What is it that makes the difference?* I wondered. *Why do some children thrive while others fail, despite the best effort of their teachers in the classroom and often in individualized remediation?* It became clear to me that these students did not start school on a level playing field with their successful peers.

It was then I realized that each child arrives on their first day of kindergarten with an Invisible Toolbox. Those who have been introduced to the world of books by being read to show up with a Toolbox overflowing with language, stories, and virtual experiences that provide a foundation for understanding the world of school and learning. They are motivated to learn to read because they *already know* there is something in it for them. Those who have not been read to also arrive with a Toolbox, but theirs is missing necessary equipment for the challenges ahead. They suffer from a deficit of language, have no idea how stories work, and lack the imaginative experiences that provide a foundation for understanding stories and the wider world they will encounter in school. They also need to be persuaded that there is something in this reading enterprise that is immediately rewarding *for them*. Because of this absence of what educators call "pre-literacy skills," learning to read is hard work.

The first day of any primary-grade school year, when the class is called to the rug for a story, the observant teacher can already distinguish the students who have been read to from those who have not. Students who have been read to walk right up and sit down expectantly, often as close to the teacher as possible. They already know that what they are about to hear will be worth their while. Children with little or no experience having been read to tend to hang back and sit on the fringes. They often have trouble listening to and following a story because they have not been trained to, and therefore have little to no expectation that what is to come is worthy of their attention.

As a new parent, understanding the importance of reading aloud to your child is as vital as all the other essential things that you learn in caring for your newborn. This knowledge is critical for our wider culture as well, because things aren't looking very hopeful on the national front when it comes to our children's reading scores. According to the 2019 NAEP, the nation's report card that periodically tests a broad cross-section of fourth and eighth grade students in the United States in both public and private schools, 65 percent of our nation's fourth graders and 66 percent of our nation's eighth graders did not score at the proficient level in reading.[1] When students do not read proficiently by the end of third grade, they're four times more likely to leave school without a diploma than their proficiently reading peers.[2] These numbers do not bode well for our nation's future or its workforce.[3]

Literacy problems have often been understood as primarily the domain of lower socio-economic classes, but statistics—and my own experience in teaching children from all backgrounds—indicate that poverty alone is not the only explanation for this crisis. Technology has had an enormous impact on families and children's readiness for school. Parents often put smart phones and tablets into the hands of their preschoolers without realizing the harm these addictive devices can cause in a child's still-developing brain. As a teacher, I can walk into a classroom and guess with great accuracy which children spend a lot of time on screens. It shows.

When I was pregnant with my son, I was given three copies of *Goodnight Moon* at various baby showers. Toward the end of my pregnancy, I began reading one of them aloud nightly to my growing belly before I dropped off to sleep. I hadn't thought too deeply about the critical importance of reading aloud before then, but as a graduate student in an educational philosophy class at Princeton

Theological Seminary, I'd learned Michael Polanyi's theory of "tacit knowing"—the idea that we understand more than we can say. The implications of that seemed enormous to me, and perhaps that is why I intuited even then that my baby was receptive at a pre-language level. At any rate, I began reading to him before birth and didn't stop until right around middle school. I didn't do it because I was hoping to set him up for an Ivy League school; I read to him because I wanted him to know the joy of books as a window to the world from the very start.

That is what reading from birth is all about. As parents, we all—regardless of where we come from—want the world for our children. We do everything we can to help them develop fully into who they are meant to be so they can have meaningful lives. Reading to them from birth—or even before—is a powerful place to start.

With my love and best wishes,

Your Child's Future Teacher

# Chapter Two

# Build It with Love

How Reading, Singing, and Speaking
to Our Babies Form the Structure
of their Invisible Toolboxes

---

Human beings are wired to connect. From the cradle
to the grave, the evidence is in that the deepest human
desire, after life itself, is the longing to connect. We
enter the world seeking it and, if we leave this world with
regrets, it is primarily because we did not love well or
deeply. The blueprint for connection is written in our cells
from the very beginning, and our understanding of this
has enormous implications for the way we parent.

For many years of human history, babies were considered
tiny bundles of relatively oblivious humanity requiring
little more than nourishment, sleep, swaddling, nappy
changes, and, in more recent times, regular visits to
the pediatrician. Twenty-first-century findings in
neuroscience, however, reveal a much more complex
picture. Brain research now shows that infants are far
more receptive and cognitively active than we previously
thought and that learning—the physical work of the brain
in forging pathways between brain cells—actually begins
in the womb. Infants, as it turns out, require much more

than physical care. The neural connections that begin to form in utero set about building an internal infrastructure that is the foundation of a child's future social, emotional, and intellectual growth. Their inborn drive to connect means that they not only desire our touch, they also want to hear from us.

Developmental psychologists have long understood the importance of bonding in healthy child development. Harry Harlow's pioneering 1930s studies with rhesus monkeys raised in isolation from their mothers and Rene Spitz's work with children orphaned in World War II revealed that emotional deprivation in the first year of life causes irreparable psychic and physical damage. Our understanding of the importance of nurturing contact has only increased with advances in neuroscience that reveal touch—which, of all our senses, has the largest sense organ—develops very early in utero. According to pediatrician Alan Greene, "At less than eight weeks, when the fetus is less than an inch long, the sense of touch is already highly developed—before there are eyes or ears."[4] An infant experiences the womb's pulsing of amniotic fluid and the contraction and expansion of its walls as a constant state of massage.[5] An infant, accustomed to this sensation of being touched and held in the womb, greatly benefits from the continuation of this experience, as touch reduces the child's level of the stress hormone cortisol.

While infant massage has long been practiced worldwide, we in the United States have only recently caught on to its importance.

Hearing is another sense that develops long before birth. According to Susan Brink, author of *The Fourth Trimester: Understanding, Nurturing, and Protecting an Infant Through the First Three Months*, the newborn, already accustomed to the sounds of the muffled maternal voice, recognizes and responds to a mother's voice first. Aside from this, the sounds of a baby's world are a meaningless din. But here is where the real learning begins:

> ...lest anyone think these undifferentiated noises are useless, think again. With an innate skill that would be the envy of a statistics student, newborns are keeping track of probabilities; setting up neural connections in response to the patterns of the words they hear. They are learning where one word ends and another begins before they utter their first da-da.[6]

Patricia Kuhl, a neuroscientist and leading expert on speech development at the University of Washington, has discovered that babies are born with the ability to hear the sound distinctions of every language that exists, but by ten months of age—maybe sooner—that ability is lost, "pruned away by a brain eager to culti-vate what will be needed and get rid of what won't."[7]

Human babies arrive in this world poised to learn.
At birth, Brink claims, babies possess:

> billions of brain cells, or neurons, but little in the way of an
> internal communication network. Immediately, every interaction
> with the world—each touch, word, smell, look—helps the baby
> lay down an infrastructure of dendrites, the branched projections
> that receive and send signals between neurons.[8]

The science that enables us to understand that infants
begin learning immediately at birth, or even before, is
clear, and its implications are profound.

But perhaps even more profound than how soon learning
begins is the beautiful metaphor that the brain cell reveals
to us, for it organically demonstrates a truth about what
it means to be human. The work of the brain at birth
is to begin making connections that enable the child to
make sense of the outside world, preparing them for their
ultimate purpose, to love. As parents, it is important
for us to understand that learning is a drive organically
rooted in a child's physical being, and its ultimate aim is
to create a meaningful life. When we speak, sing, and read
to our child from birth, this loving way of engaging builds
neural pathways in the brain that become the physical
infrastructure for all future learning and loving. Learning,
therefore, is connection, rooted in relationship.

Major religions throughout history have proclaimed a life of love as the highest human calling, and the observations of those who work in hospice care are equally compelling. Paradoxically, death often illuminates what is most important in life, and those who accompany the dying in life's final stage are privileged to bear witness to their reflections as they look back over their lives. Social worker Grace Bluerock wrote,

> For six years, I had the amazing gift of being able to experience with people their final days and weeks. For most, these last days and weeks were spent looking back over their lives in deep contemplation. Many regrets were expressed, and many tears were shed. As a hospice social worker, I got a front row seat into the lives of those precious souls as they attempted to come to terms with how they spent their time on this earth. Everyone's story was different, but each held common threads and similar regrets.[9]

The number one regret Bluerock observed in the dying during her years of service is that people wished they had loved more deeply. No one dies wishing they had made more money or worked harder. Ironically, at the moment of our departure from life, we are perhaps most conscious of the instinct that existed as an unconscious urge from the very beginning—the longing to connect.

Our very purpose is imbedded in the work of our brain cells as we enter the world, and its function is a metaphor for what we as humans are destined to do. A child's drive to connect with their parents is important to understand, as it is the foundation for all learning. From birth on, babies are at work making connections and building the mental and emotional infrastructure that will make sense of the world and carry them into life. As parents of a newborn, we are that world, and the primary responsibility to nurture this process is ours. Speaking, singing, and reading aloud honor our infant's drive to bond with us and nurture the emerging internal infrastructure that will carry them into future learning and life.

# Chapter Three

# Kindergarten and the Invisible Toolbox

## Discovering the Tools Inside

The first day of kindergarten may be one of the most emotional days in the life of a parent. Even if a child has had preschool experience, day one of kindergarten is different because it represents a child's first real launch into the wider world of school and life beyond you. It is a day marked with the ritual of new clothes, new shoes, a new lunchbox, and a first-day-of-school picture.

My son's kindergarten picture was taken at the front door of our house. Today I look at this photo of him—with his brand-spanking-new clothes and sneakers, Winnie-the-Pooh lunchbox in hand, a bright, expectant smile on his face, and one foot raised, as if poised to take a step forward—and still get a lump in my throat. I also remember my underlying anxiety that day: *Is he ready? Will his teacher be kind? Will he make friends?*

As parents, we know this is a significant day and for good reason. The launch of our child's school career that will span thirteen years has arrived, and all of the hopes, dreams, and expectations that we have for our child are wrapped up in it. As we watch them walk away from us, up the path to the kindergarten gate to their welcoming teacher, we pray that they are ready, that the experience will be wonderful, and that this day will be the first of a long and successful school career. I would venture to say that all well-meaning parents share this hope—yet there is something else in the picture of which we may not be aware. A child walks through the kindergarten gate with a lunchbox in one hand and an Invisible Toolbox in the other, and in that Toolbox there are resources that will affect their success or failure in school for years to come. By reading to your child from birth, you can ensure your child will be well equipped with these essential tools.

## Tool 1: A Rich and Large Vocabulary, the #1 Predictor of School Success

The words that a child already knows upon entering school are the building blocks that create a foundation for understanding what happens there.

According to Jim Trelease in *The Read-Aloud Handbook,*

> Yes, the child goes to school to learn new words, but the words he or she already knows determine how much of what the teacher says will be understood. And since most instruction for the first four years of school is oral, the child who has the largest vocabulary will understand the most, while the child with the smallest vocabulary will understand the least. Once reading begins, personal vocabulary feeds (or frustrates) comprehension, since school grows increasingly complicated with each grade. That's why school-entry vocabulary tests predict so accurately.[10]

A child's vocabulary grows, initially, through conversation. By fifteen months of age, a baby is able to speak first words through imitation. At two years, the average spoken word count is three hundred, and by age four, "The child already understands two-thirds to three-quarters of the words he will use in future daily life. Once he learns to talk, he'll average as many as ten words a day, not one of which is on a flash card."[11]

What accounts for the differences in vocabulary among children who enter school? The quality of spoken conversation at home is an important factor. Trelease claims that general conversation consists of five thousand commonly used words known as the Basic Lexicon. Beyond those are five thousand more words that are known and understood, yet used less often, known as the Common Lexicon. Beyond these ten thousand words are the "rare words" that don't often crop up in daily use or conversation, but which play a critical role in reading.[12] A child's familiarity with the "rare words" profoundly affects reading comprehension, and they are most commonly found in printed text, not in conversation nor television nor movies. Children whose vocabulary exposure has been limited to conversation or screens are at a distinct disadvantage from their peers who have been immersed in stories in print through having been read to. Because learning increases exponentially, this deficit is rarely made up as a child grows older.

## Tool 2: An Attraction to Books

Children who arrive at school having been read to possess another key factor for success; they come to school familiar with the rewards of reading. They do not need to be taught or convinced that reading is a worthwhile endeavor because, having been immersed in stories, they already know this to be true. My son's first-grade teacher had a classroom filled with picture books and kept an expansive and attractive display set up on bookshelves that invited exploration. On day one, she could spot the children who had been read to because they would make a beeline for those books upon entering her classroom. They were attracted to them as bees are to honey, for they already knew there was *something in it for them.* Learning to read comes much more easily for them than for their peers with empty Toolboxes, who must not only become convinced of its pleasures, but also must play catch-up and work with their teachers to develop the rest of the tools not yet in their possession.

## Tool 3: An Intuitive Understanding of How Books Work

There are a number of important skills about the way books work that children need to understand in order to learn to read. Children arrive at school with this knowledge if they have been read to: we begin at the front of the book and read to the back; we start at the top of the page and read to the bottom; we read the words from left to right. Pictures give us clues about what is happening in the story that the words may not tell us. They also begin to intuit that symbols on the page stand for sounds that become words. Children with no experience with books arrive at school already behind in understanding this rudimentary yet essential information.

## Tool 4: A Well-Developed Attention Span

Children who have been read to also already know how to attend to what is important, for listening to stories has trained them to do so. These are the children who cluster at the feet of their teacher on the rug when it's story time. They are better able to focus visually and aurally than their peers who have not been read to and can easily shut out extraneous distractions in their environment. I have often observed young students who have little experience being read to choosing to sit on the periphery of the group, their gazes wandering around the room instead of zeroing in on the story. They have difficulty following along and often aren't able to answer simple questions about it. These children are not unable to do so, they simply lack the motivation and training to listen and mentally focus. The lap of a loving parent is the best place to learn how to pay attention.

## Tool 5: Confidence and Expressive Reading and Speaking

Children who have been read to by an adult who reads expressively will also become expressive oral readers themselves through imitation. Good oral reading is very difficult to teach. It's a skill I continue to emphasize in my fifth-grade literature classes, but for some students, reading aloud with varied tone and feeling is challenging. It does not come naturally to them, as it does to those who have been so immersed in expressive reading that it's the only way they know *how* to read aloud. Walk into any classroom and listen to students reading aloud from a text, and when you hear a student who reads mechanically in a monotone, it's likely this child was read to very little early on. When parents model expressive reading aloud, children internalize tone, inflection, and emotion intuitively and will naturally read aloud this way themselves. This will show up in their comfort and confidence in reading and speaking throughout their school lives and beyond.

## Tool 6: Foundations for Good Writing, Grammar, and Spelling

Another item in the Toolbox that sets a child up for success is an innate understanding of how stories are constructed. All narratives have a structure: a beginning, middle, and end. They also have conflict. The protagonist wants something, but there is an obstacle that must be overcome in order to achieve the "want" and for the story to resolve. Children who have been exposed to many stories come to school with an unconscious understanding of this structure. Not only the broader shape of stories, but patterns in sentences—the building blocks of stories— become part of the child's internal landscape. This quality, along with the vocabulary and imagination that are developed through reading aloud, sets children up to be successful writers because understanding how words are put together to form sentences is no mystery. Enthusiastic readers possess the tools to become the best writers.

One Back to School Night, my son's seventh-grade English teacher threw a question out to all of us parents: "What do you think is the number one way for your child to improve their spelling?" Many volunteered answers. Paying attention in class. Studying. Making flash cards. The teacher shook his head. Nope. All good things to do, but not the most important. "The number one way to improve in spelling," he informed us, "is to read."

What this middle school teacher understood was that continued immersion in words creates visual memory maps in the brain. The greater the exposure to words, the more likely a student will be able to not only identify a correctly spelled word, but actually produce it as well. In the same way, children who arrive at school on the first day having heard many words will be more likely to recognize words when they read them, use them with facility when writing, and ultimately be able to spell them.

Quite simply, immersion in stories develops a child's capacity for language and how it is used. As a teacher of writing, I've witnessed this truth again and again. Students who have been read to and who read themselves have a plethora of riches to draw upon when it comes time to set pencil to paper. Children who have not struggle to write because those neurological connections have not yet been made.

## Tool 7: Access to a Wider World—
## A Requisite for Understanding What Is Read

Reading aloud fills a child's Toolbox with another tool that is critical for success: the background of experiences and exposure that is necessary for understanding what is read. Stories expand the boundaries of a child's world in the best possible way. Maine is a place with evergreen trees and blueberries growing wild, which bears love. How does a child in Southern California know this without reading Robert McCloskey's *Blueberries for Sal*? That same child might never come across a snow angel without exposure to *The Snowy Day* by Ezra Jack Keats. The reading a child does in school is filled with myriad references that fall outside their natural orbit, and their degree of familiarity with them will determine their ability to understand what they read. Reading aloud to a child expands not only their world of words, but also their grasp of the world itself.

The background of experiences and exposure that comes through reading will impact a child's success in school in all subjects. The ability to understand and appreciate word problems in math, concepts in science, and stories and places in history are all predicated on the background of knowledge a child brings to each of these studies.

A former student of mine happened to be a geography whiz. Each year, Brian plowed through the competition in our school-wide National Geographic Geography Bee and would go on to compete at the state level. But his success was not due to hours spent poring over maps and atlases, as one might think. In fact, he never studied to prepare for these competitions. His incredible breadth of knowledge about geography had come about another way. Brian was a military history enthusiast and read voraciously on the subject. Indirectly, he had acquired expertise in geography due to his extensive reading. His story illustrates the manifold and unexpected rewards of reading because it demonstrates the interconnectedness of all learning.

When reading, the child's firing neurons are building connections and creating branches into new territories of which they might not even be aware, which will not only expand their knowledge, but also impact their ability to grasp future learning in diverse arenas.

## Tool 8: The Ability to Find Joy— Anytime, Anywhere

The child who loves reading or being read to will never be bored. The portability of books means that, as a parent, you can take them with you wherever you go, and they can be pulled out at a moment's notice whenever you find you have time—or the need for comfort—on your hands.

I'll never forget the first time we traveled with our son, who was just seven months of age. He endured a flight from Southern California to Colorado and then a long shuttle ride from the airport to our destination before becoming fussy. I was as concerned about the strangers sharing our airport shuttle having to listen to an unhappy baby in close quarters as I was about my little guy's misery. Fortunately, I had one of his favorite books handy. I pulled out his copy of *Hands, Hands, Fingers, Thumbs* by P. D. Eastman and began reading softly. His crying stopped immediately, and he was enthralled by its silly but catchy rhythm. Book over, he immediately started wailing again. So I cracked the book and started all over, "Hands, hands, fingers, thumb...dum-ditty-dum-ditty, dum-dum-dum!" and he quieted once again, listening attentively. My husband and I traded off, rereading the book countless times before we reached our destination. It was an exhausting effort, but I'll always be grateful to

P. D. Eastman for saving us all on that long ride from the airport. I'm sure it drove the other passengers in the shuttle slightly mad to have to listen to this ditty multiple times, but I was convinced it would have been more painful for all concerned if my son had cried his way to Estes Park.

Likewise, when your child is older and can read on their own, they need never be bored. When there is "nothing to do, no one to play with," there are always books they can turn to. As literature professor Mason Cooley said, "Books give us someplace to go when we have to stay where we are." Children who learn the pleasure of reading will carry the ability to entertain themselves, to learn, and to continue growing intellectually and emotionally right on into adulthood.

## Tool 9: An Expanded Imagination and Intellectual Curiosity

Children who are read to also acquire imagination and intellectual curiosity, essential qualities for learning and creation. Neuroscience has recently shed new light on the neurological effects of reading, proving that stories stimulate the brain in ways we have not previously understood and even change how we behave in life.[13] We have long understood that reading stimulates the language processing areas of the brain, but brain scans now show many other cortexes are stimulated as well.

Studies reveal that highly sensory language, the type of language found in fiction, triggers brain activity outside the language processing zones. Words like "lavender" or "cinnamon" elicit activity in the olfactory or smelling area of the brain. Metaphors like "He had leathery hands," which evokes texture, stimulate the sensory cortex. Reading about movement, likewise, can affect the motor cortex.[14] This certainly explains my own reading experience. How many times has a descriptive passage about, for the sake of example, a mouthwatering piece of dark chocolate cake prompted me to put my novel down and head to the kitchen to see if I can find some because I can practically already taste it?

According to Annie Murphy Paul, author of *Origins: How the Nine Months Before Birth Shape the Rest of Our Lives*, "The brain...does not make much of a distinction between reading about an experience and encountering it in real life; in each case, the same neurological regions are stimulated."[15] When a parent reads stories to a child, the child does not just learn *about* the world of the story, they *experience* the world of the story.

As a child's knowledge grows, their curiosity and enthusiasm to know more is stimulated. Teachers know that students who read for pleasure will be their most intellectually curious students. Each year I teach a unit on Greek mythology to my fifth graders. While studying *D'aulaires' Book of Greek Myths* is a high-interest endeavor for just about everyone, I've observed that students who have read the Percy Jackson and the Olympians series before our study are the most enthusiastic and engaged of all. Why? Because of their prior reading, these students bring knowledge they've gained to our work that makes them hungry for more. These are the students with their hands up, excitedly pointing out discrepancies between the versions of the myths we are reading and the stories they have already read, filling us in on the backstories we may not be familiar with, and voraciously reading beyond us. One student memorably went on to tackle *The Iliad* for his pleasure reading as we wrapped up our class study.

The child who has been read to arrives at school with not only a greater knowledge base than their peer who has not been read to, but a greater experience base, an expanded capacity to imagine, and the crown jewel: intellectual curiosity, or the intrinsic desire to know more.

## Tool 10: Empathy and the Ability to Understand Others

Studies also show that reading fiction develops the capacity for empathy. As we enter the world of the story, not only the experiences, but also the characters become real for us. At a neurological level, we live vicariously through them, putting ourselves into the shoes of the characters.

The brain networks that are used to understand stories are the same networks used to understand social interactions with others. "Narratives offer a unique opportunity to engage this capacity, as we identify with characters' longings and frustrations, guess at their hidden motives, and track their encounters with friends and enemies, neighbors and lovers."[16] Psychologists call the capacity that we have to understand the feelings and actions of others "theory of mind." A 2010 study with preschoolers by Dr. Raymond Mar of York University in Canada determined that the more stories the children had read to them, the greater their theory of mind, or "their ability to attribute mental states—beliefs, intents, desires, pretending, knowledge, etc.—to oneself and others and to understand that others have beliefs, desires, and intentions that are different from one's own."[17] A capacity to understand others who are different from oneself and to empathize with them is an important tool that is essential not only for school, but for life.

Having read to groups of children hundreds of times over the years, I remain astonished when I witness even a very young child's ability to analyze a character's feelings and behavior during story time. Children who have been read to not only have the capacity to imaginatively enter the world of a character; they also have the language and vocabulary to express their opinions. In short, children who have been read to learn how to think and feel and express themselves.

***

The Invisible Toolbox may be unseen, but its contents have a far-reaching impact on a child's readiness to navigate the world of school. Reading aloud to a child from birth fills the Toolbox with an ever-expanding vocabulary that stretches beyond the realm of everyday conversation and screens, a positive expectation for the world of school, practical knowledge of how books function, a greater attention span, expressive reading and speaking, an innate understanding of how stories work and how sentences are constructed that will impact their future writing, grammar, and spelling abilities, the background of knowledge that is necessary for reading comprehension, the ability to enjoy oneself anytime and anywhere, an expanded imagination and intellectual curiosity, and empathy.

It is this last dividend, the capacity for empathy, that is the key to understanding the most important reason for reading aloud to a child.

# Chapter Four

# The Greatest Gift of the Invisible Toolbox, or Why We *Really* Read

## Awakening the Inner Life of Your Child

Reading aloud from birth on to facilitate a child's potential in school is a noble endeavor, but there is an even more fundamental reason for doing so. The most important reason for reading aloud from infancy onward is to nurture the parent-child bond, which is the critical foundation for emotional intelligence, well-being, and success in learning and life. Spending a few minutes each day reading aloud to a child can be a means to that end. According to an article from the WestED Center for Prevention and Early Intervention, California's Infant, Preschool, and Family Mental Health Initiative, "Social and emotional development is the foundation for how children learn and this development begins in infancy."[18] The context of reading aloud, then, which is the parent-child relationship, is the key to a child's foundation for growth.

We have already learned that from birth an infant immediately seeks connection. The brain, which begins to make connections to understand the world, is learning from the very start, and the child's success at doing so is entirely dependent upon the responsiveness of its parent. The quality of parenting and its impact on a child is further illuminated in the same article:

> What happens in these [parent-child] relationships and the messages infants receive about themselves is the source of their social and emotional health. Are people caring and consistent? Is the world a safe and stable place? Are people attuned to the infant's unique needs? Recent research has confirmed that the optimum development of an infant's social and emotional health hinges on the responses of and relationships with their caregivers.[19]

Our ability to be that consistent, responsive caregiver is critical, and it's essential for us as parents to reflect upon and understand in light of our own family history. As parents, we inevitably draw upon what we experienced in our own family of origin. If we were so fortunate as to have parents who were responsive and present to us, we will become the same kind of parent because it is what we know. If we were not so fortunate, having a child becomes our opportunity to understand our own experience and learn new ways of being for ourselves and for our child.

A child's physical requirements for nutrition, health, hygiene, and sleep are most easily tuned into, and having them met is essential for emotional health. But the development of emotional health extends beyond simply meeting a child's physical needs. Developing emotional health also requires that parents connect with their child's inner world, an intuitive experience that involves being present, enjoying the child, and connecting with and affirming their feelings. In order for a parent to be able to do this, we must, of course, be in touch with our own inner world.

Why is connecting with our child's inner world important? The inner world of the child is the source of self and their motivation to discover who they are in relation to the outside world. Even at three months of age, the infant will regularly respond to the image of a face, which is symbolic of communication and presence.[20] It is no wonder that we as parents instinctively gaze into the infant's face with exaggerated smiles and cooing, in hopes of eliciting a response. The impetus to connect is intuitive, yet it must continue to be cultivated through all stages of the child's development, as it will profoundly affect future learning and growth in school and beyond.

Reading aloud nurtures the parent-child connection. When reading aloud is part of a daily family routine, it provides a steady point of connection both parent and child can look forward to and count on. Practicing this daily ritual communicates not only that reading is important, but that *the child* is important. Snuggling and cuddling up together with a book creates feelings of warmth and can even provide a bit of an oasis from daily pressures and burdens.

My son's father and I divorced when he was quite young, and our nightly story-time ritual meant a great deal to us both during those difficult days. One winter evening, a friend of mine from high school was visiting from out of town. After dinner and his bath, my five-year-old son trotted downstairs in his footed blue pj's, a book tucked under his arm. He marched right over to my friend, who had settled into a rocking chair by the fire, and politely instructed her that she would have to move. A bit startled, she asked why.

"Because my mom and I have to toast our toes by the fire," he answered matter-of-factly.

"Toasting our toes by the fire" was code for our nightly ritual of snuggling up in the rocker by the fireplace and reading together, and my son was not about to let anything or anyone interfere with this. Our ritual was such a source of comfort and security for him that even the novelty of having overnight company paled next to this important routine. The warmth and closeness of cuddling together with a book at the end of a long day meant just as much to me.

When a parent not only reads a story aloud, but also invites their child to interact with it, children receive the greatest benefits.[21] At a very young age, this might mean asking a child to point to a picture, commenting on the pictures yourself, asking questions, discussing what is happening, and inquiring what they are thinking about. This type of engagement enables the child and parent to reflect together and opens the doors between the parent's and the child's inner worlds. *What are you thinking? What are you feeling? What did you notice?* Conversations about the books you share together teach your child to be aware of and give expression to their feelings.

Reading aloud to a child to awaken and support their inner life is about assuring them that they, at the core of their being, are valued and important—and this requires our greatest attention and respect, as it will have consequences far into the future.

# Chapter Five

# The Parent's Toolbox

## How You Can Become Your Child's First Reading Teacher, Get Past the Hurdles, and Enjoy the Treasures Inside

We are our child's first reading teachers. Our relationship to books—not what we say about them, but how we actually relate to them—is what children learn. Do we enjoy reading ourselves? Is it something we do every day? If the answer is yes, then we already have one of the most important tools needed to introduce our children to the joys of reading. But what if we struggled with reading ourselves? What if we don't like to read? What if there are cost constraints and language barriers? Here are some tools to keep in mind for your very own toolbox.

## Tool 1: Parent Yourself

Parents who struggled with reading as children or who have never really discovered its pleasures for themselves may feel helpless or ill-equipped to lead. My advice to them is that this is not only your child's golden opportunity to grow; this is your opportunity as well. One of parenting's greatest benefits is having the chance to rework or recover experiences that we may have missed out on in our own childhoods. Do not misunderstand; I'm not promoting the type of vicarious living we see on the Little League field when overly aggressive parents relive their dreams of baseball glory through their children. The benefits I refer to have to do with the fact that when we raise children they open up new experiences to us through the worlds they are drawn to. This can happen with reading as well. If your experience with reading was difficult or unremarkable, doing right by your child gives you an opportunity to rework and overcome that. It is never too late to parent yourself as well as your child.

I was an avid reader as a child, but my interests were quite narrow, and I rarely read outside my comfort zone. For a period of time, all I read and reread were my beloved Trixie Belden mysteries, and I missed out on many classics that I'm sure I would have loved had I received encouragement to break out of my detective mode. As my son grew up and we read together, I got my second chance to experience some of these unread greats. I remember reading The Boxcar Children stories together when he was in preschool, the remarkable Oz books by Frank L. Baum when he was in kindergarten, and the hilarious Great Brain series when he was in second grade. I know I enjoyed them as much as he did.

It's important that read-aloud time is a mutually enjoyable activity. The best of children's literature has universal age appeal because it speaks to the child in all of us. Sharing books with your child is your chance to enjoy these treasures too.

## Tool 2: Get a Library Card
## and Get to Know Your Local Bookstore

One's economic situation does not have to limit the ability to lead a child into reading. When I was newly divorced and my son was young, money was tight and I couldn't afford to buy as many books as I would have liked. The books that I did buy I purchased inexpensively through the *Scholastic Book Club* flyers available through his preschool, but most of our books at that time came from our local public library. We began making weekly trips to the library when he was a toddler, attending story time there, and regularly returning home with stacks of books. The children's section of the library is a very friendly place. Twenty years later, I still have sweet memories of being tucked up together on the carpet, reading *Curious George*. We checked out the entire series over the course of one summer. Another time, when he was going through his dinosaur phase, we read both fiction and nonfiction. Right alongside him, I learned to identify and pronounce the names of all the dinosaurs.

The children's section of your local bookstore can also be an inviting place to hang out and read together. Bookstores often host book signings and author events that are totally free. Nothing beats meeting your favorite author in person.

Ideally, it is beneficial to have books in the home, and I highly recommend it. But what is really important is our attitude toward books and our access to them. When our children see us read, when we read to them, and when we make it a priority to provide them with books on a regular basis by visiting the library or bookstore or ordering through clubs or online, we are providing the best possible foundation for their intellectual and emotional growth.

## Tool 3: Don't Let Language Barriers Stop You

Parents with limited English need not despair either. The library, along with online providers, offers audiobooks that can be checked out or downloaded and shared with your child. One day, a boy in my fifth-grade literature class shared that his father was reading *Little House on the Prairie*. In class, I often spoke about and recommended important books that should not be missed, and this boy would go home and tell his parents about them. Inevitably, these titles would make it onto the reading list of his father. I was impressed by this man's eagerness to expand his knowledge, not only of his adopted country's new language, but also its literature and history. The modeling he did for his son about what is important was priceless. This student invariably made outstanding choices in his own pleasure reading and became an excellent writer.

## Tool 4: Learn to Find Time for Reading When You Don't Seem to Have Any

Twenty-four hours often doesn't seem long enough for all that we have to do these days. Finding time to sit down and read to your child—or for yourself—may seem impossible in the midst of the crush of responsibilities that many of us carry. Our challenge is to find a way to fit reading aloud into a pleasurable routine that reenergizes and is looked forward to. Like any new habit, it may require some effort at first, but once established, reading is an activity that won't feel like "just one more thing I have to do." Its rewards are such that you and your child will eagerly anticipate this time together.

Establishing a regular time that can be counted on from day to day is important. As you may recall from the "we're going to toast our toes by the fire" story, my son and I read nightly after his bath time and before bed. This was ideal for us, as we were both winding down from the day. The "must-dos" of the day were generally behind us, so we were both relaxed enough to snuggle down into the sofa, in a rocking chair, or on his bunk bed and lose ourselves together in a good story.

One of the reasons I love to read aloud as a ritual before bedtime is that it's a chance to reconnect after either being apart or simply after the busyness of the day.

Talking about the story may even elicit conversations with your child that might not emerge otherwise, as it can be a springboard for sharing our own lives. When that happens, it's magic; if not, the simple joy of cuddling up together and enjoying a good book is its own reward that will create memories for you both that will last a lifetime.

Bedtime may be ideal, but it need not be the only time for reading together. Keeping books in the car or in your bag can be handy for those times when you find yourselves out and about waiting—for the doctor, for a sibling's baseball practice to end, or for the line in the grocery store to move along. It's much more advantageous to share a book than to hand your child a phone or an iPad to pass the time. The pattern of your family's day will determine the best times for you.

## Tool 5: Enjoy the Greatest Reward of All: Connection

Once you've established the practice of daily reading with your child, you will find the greatest reward of all is the connection established between you. Yes, you will enjoy wonderful stories together and will be entertained and transported by them, but the best part of all is that you'll be sharing the experience together and learn more about each other. When you select books to read together, you discover what your child's interests and emotional needs are. A preschooler on a roll with the Curious George series may be looking not only to laugh, but to be reassured that, even when they make mistakes, they're still loved, forgiven, and all will come out right in the end. When you share books of your choosing—perhaps books that you enjoyed as a child or books you wished you'd read but missed—your child learns about you as well.

Once your child is off to school, learns to read, and grows up, their knowledge and interests will take off. I remember shaking my head constantly during the adolescent years at my son's ever-expanding world of knowledge and interests: *Where did you learn that?* I'd wonder. For the longest time, we are the world for our child and so have some idea of what that world encompasses. And then one day, surprise! Your child's world has grown far beyond you, and they are now reading and learning in uncharted waters of which you may know little. And this, once again, is your opportunity to grow. My son has taught me more about history than I would ever have discovered on my own and piqued my interest in such a way that I'm now a voracious reader of World War I- and World War II-era fiction and nonfiction.

Infectious enthusiasm for a subject can work both ways, benefitting both parent and child. For many years I've taught a nonfiction literature unit on Robert Ballard's compelling narrative of his discovery of the greatest of all shipwrecks, *Exploring the Titanic*. One year during our study, a student in my class who tended to be academically unmotivated and an indifferent reader began to stay after class and share her excitement with me about what she was now reading at home. As it turned out, her mother had a personal connection to and interest in the *Titanic* story, and together the two of them were reading the memoir of a stewardess who survived not only the sinking of the *Titanic*, but two other shipwrecks as well. It was clear to me that my student's curiosity and motivation to learn and share were directly impacted by her mother's enthusiasm. I was thrilled to see the light in her eyes and realized, once again, the power that we have as parents to ignite it simply by sharing our time and genuine interest in a book.

# Chapter Six

# How to Read Aloud to Your Child

## From Birth through Adolescence

Parents can nurture the parent-child bond and inspire a passion for reading from the very beginning. The American Academy of Pediatrics recommends reading aloud daily from birth, but a parent may wish to begin before, for the sense of hearing is developing in utero. Regardless of when you begin reading aloud to your child, the most important thing is to have fun and enjoy it.

Parents of older elementary students who have not read much to their child will occasionally ask if it is too late to begin. My answer is a resounding *no*. In the years before adolescence, the time and attention that parents give to their children is powerful and magnetic. If you as a parent can find a book or series that engages you both, you will inspire the imagination and motivation of your child, and it can have a positive effect on their attitude toward school.

Although it is never too late to begin sharing books with your child, reading from birth—or even before—is the ideal place to start.

## Before Birth

What is important to appreciate at this stage is that your baby's sense of hearing begins to develop in utero. Your understanding of your child's growing awareness is important here, and you can begin to nurture your bond in a variety of ways:

- Speak to your child.
- Sing.
- Read simple picture books or nursery rhymes aloud.
- Play classical or soft relaxing music.

It may be helpful to create a small daily ritual for a specific time in your day when you focus on connecting with your growing baby. This can help to lay the foundation for having a daily time of reading later on, when your baby arrives. When I began reading aloud nightly to my son in the later stages of my pregnancy, it enhanced my awareness of him as an individual soon to be apart from me.

## Infancy

Now that your baby has arrived, it will seem at first that all they do is sleep and eat. But remember, your little one knows your voice and their brain is now working to distinguish sounds.

I am convinced that babies understand feelings and tone of voice before they understand our words. When my son was in this stage, I had the distinct impression that he understood *something*, and so I behaved as if he did by talking with him. I remember that he would watch me and listen attentively. If I were folding sheets from the dryer, I would tell him about what I was doing and maybe even describe how crisp they felt or how fresh they smelled. It may sound silly, but if you think about it, *everything* is new to your baby and they are curious about everything— even something as mundane as bedsheets. Talking with your baby not only teaches language, it teaches them that they are important and worthy of your attention and communication.

As a routine of eating, napping, and sleeping through the night eventually emerges, you can begin to create a daily routine that includes reading aloud. In the meantime, with sensitivity to your baby's moods and wakefulness, you can:

- Speak to them as if they understand you.

- Sing to your baby.

- Chant poems or nursery rhymes.

- Begin to establish a nightly ritual of reading a story aloud before bedtime.

- Cuddle your baby.

## Older Baby and Toddlerhood

Your baby is growing quickly and becoming increasingly alert. During this stage, they will begin mimicking sounds, speaking their first words, and expanding their motor skills. As the latter happens, it may seem impossible to get them to sit still long enough to read a story. Don't despair. Your child does not have to be sitting in your lap in order for you to read to them. If they wriggle off your lap to explore a toy, you can keep right on reading. To encourage cuddle time while reading, however, it is best to catch your busy mover when they are in a less active mode. A great time for snuggling while reading is right after the evening bath before bed. Just after waking from a nap is also a prime time for reading and cuddling, as it makes for a comforting transition from sleep to wakefulness.

If you have not done so already, be sure to introduce nursery rhymes to your child during this stage. Children of this age love the repetition, the rhyme, the wordplay, and the surprises of these classic verses and will want to hear them over and over. They will delight your child as they build critical pre-reading skills such as recognizing rhyming words. Elementary teachers everywhere can tell you of their despair that parents no longer share nursery rhymes with their children. One school year, "Little Bo Peep" came up somehow in a discussion in my upper elementary literature class, and I got mostly blank stares from my students. I proceeded to recite the entire rhyme for them—to more blank stares and puzzled looks. *Please* read them to your child.

- Speak to your older baby/toddler in a way that respects your child's growing ability to understand the feeling or tone of your words and the words themselves.

- Sing with, chant nursery rhymes to, and play with your child.

- Add another daily reading time to your nightly reading ritual before bed, if possible.

- While reading, ask your child questions they can answer by pointing to pictures; board books and books with tactile features like *Pat the Bunny* and *Pat the Cat* are appealing and engaging at this stage.

- Build your child's personal library. (If money is an issue, explore secondhand bookstores or library book sales. Register your child with Dolly Parton's Imagination Library, a free monthly distribution program.)

- Begin regular visits to your local public library; attend children's story-time offerings.

- Support your local bookstore. Children's book authors often visit for readings and signings. These events are free.
- Continue cuddling.

## The Preschool Years

You may be astonished to observe your child's swiftly expanding vocabulary at this stage of life. If you have been reading to your child regularly, their vocabulary is now growing at a rapid rate. Their ability to sit and listen to increasingly complex stories is growing as well. Picture books and even some chapter books will be appropriate and appealing now. It is important to follow your child's interests and lead on the types of stories you share. A child's interest is usually a good gauge of what they are ready for developmentally. Acquaint yourself with recommendations from the children's section of your public library, and get to know the librarians there so that you can introduce your child to a wide variety of literature that is developmentally appropriate. Spend time browsing the children's section of your local bookstore with your preschooler. Online resources with age-appropriate recommendations, along with the resources listed at the back of this book, may be helpful as well. Don't worry if your child becomes enamored with and only wants to read about a particular subject or series for a time. That is to be expected and is actually a good thing because it reveals intellectual curiosity. Much of what you do at this stage is to continue to build upon the foundation you have already created.

- Sing, chant, recite, and read nursery rhymes together.

- Play together.

- Continue your daily story times, if possible, and nightly ritual of reading aloud together before bedtime.

- Discuss the stories you read together; ask your child questions as they occur to you; encourage your preschooler to make predictions; teach your child to find personal connections between the story and their everyday life experiences by sharing your own connections to the story. For example, while reading aloud the autobiographical picture book *The Art Lesson* by Tomie de Paola, I might share that the boy in the story reminds me of a boy from my kindergarten class, Paul Picarello, who amazed us all with his expert dinosaur drawings.

- Continue regular weekly visits to your public library, and let your child choose and carry home their own stack of books.

- Continue to build your child's personal library; if your child attends preschool and their teacher participates in the *Scholastic Reading Club*, you will find ordering books through the club an excellent opportunity to build your child's library and encourage their growing love of books.

- Keep cuddling.

## The Elementary Years

Your child may begin to express an interest in decoding words and start to read in preschool, kindergarten, or first grade, depending on their personality and the curriculum of the school in which they're enrolled. If you and your child are enjoying daily reading together, your child will likely step into reading smoothly when they are developmentally ready because you have filled their Invisible Toolbox and laid the foundation of necessary pre-literacy skills.

I did not teach my son to read before he started school. We visited the library regularly, read together daily, and I enrolled him in a preschool program that did not stress academics, but emphasized socialization and play. His kindergarten program taught readiness, but not reading explicitly, so when he began first grade he was not reading independently. Within the first month or so of first grade he was, and by January he was reading at an advanced level and surpassed peers who had been encouraged to read independently much earlier through attending academically oriented preschools. I am convinced that this is because his Invisible Toolbox was overflowing. Once the skill of decoding words was unlocked for him, he literally exploded into reading. I will always be grateful that those fleeting years before elementary school were filled with water play, digging in the sand, make-believe, swinging in a tire swing, listening to lots and lots of stories, and the joy and freedom of playing with his friends.

Unfortunately, today most preschools emphasize academics, teaching children their letters and sounds and how to write, and the kindergarten curriculum now is the first-grade curriculum of a decade or so ago. Our national anxiety about education and obsession with testing is forcing our children to speed up their academic growth in a way that is not developmentally sound. When we put achievement ahead of the love of learning, we invert our priorities; for when love of learning is the primary goal, achievement will naturally follow. Down the road, we will undoubtedly see a backlash for these misguided policies.

As parents, the best thing that we can do for our children in a climate such as this is to continue to connect with them and read to them. The full Toolbox is the best way to prepare your child for what lies ahead. Through these years, you will continue to be amazed at your child's expanding vocabulary and growing intellectual curiosity because of the talking and reading you do together, and because of the books that they can now read on their own.

- Continue your nightly routine of reading aloud and discussing what you read together. Your child will be able to comprehend aurally far beyond what he can read independently during these years, so introduce the classics, such as *Black Beauty*, *Treasure Island*, *The Adventures of Tom Sawyer*. This is the way a child gains a powerful vocabulary without having to work hard for it.

- Develop creative ways to read aloud together. For example, you could read all the narration, while your child reads the dialogue.

- Ask your child about and share together the school's required reading list. Some of my most successful literature students have parents who always read our assigned books as well, so that they can discuss them with their child. This is not only a great help for your child academically, but it's a way of staying connected with your child and their world.

- Continue to help your child build their personal library. It will change during these years as they outgrow certain books and add others. When it was time for us to cull my son's library, we boxed up the special ones and put them away and donated the rest.

- Continue to visit the library and your local bookstore regularly.

- Keep cuddling and talking to your child about their reading, their thoughts and feelings, their day.

## The Adolescent Years

The adolescent years can be trying ones, as your child navigates their growing independence and need to separate from you and forge their own identity. If you have created a foundation of connection and shared love of books, it can help to carry you through these potentially challenging years. You may feel that your child's rate of growth, intellectually and verbally, has surpassed you due to all the independent reading they are doing.

While it may seem that the time for reading aloud together is over, it doesn't have to be. Each September at Back to School Night, parents of my fifth-grade students are often surprised that I recommend they read aloud to their children—or begin again if they have stopped. I explain that doing so not only helps their children in all the ways we have discussed so far in this book, but also serves to help them stay connected as their children are entering pre-adolescence and developmentally preparing to separate. One mother shared with me later in the school year that she had taken my advice to heart and created a nightly read-aloud ritual with her two sons, one a fifth grader, the other a seventh grader. She reported that the boys were enthusiastic about it, and she found it to be a great way to keep their connection flowing as they entered adolescence.

Sometimes the uncharted waters your child explores may include independent reading choices that make you uncomfortable. Recently, a friend took her teenage granddaughter to buy a book for a summer reading assignment. She was required to read a nonfiction book, but was free to choose her own title, so she chose a book torn right out of the headlines, the disturbing story of three young women who had been abducted and kept for years by a mentally ill man. My friend's first instinct was to tell her granddaughter, "No. This is not an appropriate book"—but she held her tongue. Instead, she made herself available to her granddaughter, and they had daily discussions about the story as she read it. What a rich gift my friend gave her granddaughter. Had she refused to buy the book, her granddaughter might have found a way to read it anyway, but she would have missed the opportunity to share her feelings and questions with a caring adult. Our presence and support are the bedrock of our children's resilience as they grow in their understanding of the world.

- Old routines may be difficult to hang onto during these years, but rest assured, the foundation of relationship and love of books that you have built will remain.

- Continue showing interest in and discussing books that your adolescent is choosing to read independently or is assigned to read at school; read them yourself if you can, so that you can have deeper conversations.

- Nightly ritual read-alouds may be a thing of the past during these years, but also may have turned into family read-alouds that encompass several ages of children; your child may now have his own nightly ritual of reading in bed before sleeping.

- Continue to support your child's growing personal library.

- Continue to encourage regular library visits.

- Keep cuddling—as allowed—and listen and talk to your adolescent.

## Post-Childhood

Reading becomes a way of life for the young adult who has been read to from infancy. The young person who reads books and does not rely solely on screens for news, information, and entertainment will not only never be at a loss for pleasure, but will bring much-needed leadership to whatever endeavor they turn their hand to, in their work life and in our culture at large. The influence that an informed, literate person can have is needed now, more than ever, in all walks of life.

My son is now a young adult and does not live with me, but every time we are together, our conversation includes books. *What are you reading?* we ask each other, and sometimes we trade books back and forth. Our conversations about books are one of our most meaningful ways of connecting now that he is grown, and I know they will continue to be because the love of reading is central to who we are individually and foundational to our bond.

Reading from birth forges a foundation of relationship and love of reading that has implications far into the future. It will impact both you and your child intellectually, emotionally, and spiritually in ways far beyond what you can imagine.

# Chapter Seven

# Important Dos and Don'ts

## DO Talk, Read, and Sing to Your Baby Right from the Start

Because hearing is the most highly developed sense at birth, your baby is tuned in to you right from the start. It may not look like much is going on, but the neurons in your baby's brain are already at work, making connections and actively distinguishing sounds. And remember, the love you communicate through your sounds, touch, and good will is unequivocally understood.

## DON'T Plug into Devices Too Soon

The American Academy of Pediatrics advises *no screen time at all* for children under the age of two. Studies indicate that reading an actual book with a young child is more advantageous because parents who do so tend to be more interactive, engaging their child in discussion about the story. When reading with a device, parents and children focus more on it than the story itself. With the bells and whistles that children's e-books now include, a shift in focus occurs, to the detriment of the experience that could be building language skills. What is important in the read-aloud experience is the interaction that transpires between the parent and child, not between the child and the screen.[22]

I think of how much easier it would have been for me to quiet my fussy seven-month-old on that long shuttle ride to Estes Park from the airport, if it had happened today, by pulling out my iPhone and logging onto *Little Baby Bum* instead of reading his favorite picture book over and over again. This nursery-themed program happens to be, as of this writing, the ninth most popular YouTube channel—a concerning statistic when you consider its target audience. Its staggering popularity attests to how tempting it can be to simply prop a baby in front of a screen tuned in to this "age-appropriate" entertainment. Ease and convenience, however, are no substitute for the nurturing that happens when a parent engages with their child through books.

With older children reading independently, studies are also indicating advantages to reading traditional books over e-readers, particularly at bedtime. A team at Harvard Medical School found that light emitted from e-readers had a physiological impact on teenage readers and interrupted their sleep cycles.[23]

My own observation is that there is simply great value in the tangible nature of an actual book that affects sensory memory. The tactile sensation of holding a particular book in hand—its shape, heft, and texture—become imbedded in the memory of reading the book itself. We experience spotting a familiar well-loved book on a shelf and thumbing through it again differently from the way we experience browsing a virtual bookshelf on an iPad or Kindle. With an e-reader, we lose the sensory experience of the book even if that book has sounds or interactive touch. For children, especially, the ability to hold a book in hand, page through it, and return to it again and again without a mediating device is essential. Experiencing a book in this way also builds the necessary understanding of how we read: front to back, left to right, and top to bottom.

# DO Monitor Your Older Child's Use of Technology

Technology is an important and unavoidable part of our lives, but setting limits on your child's involvement with it is critical. The titans of technology, who understand how powerfully addicting devices can be, employ very strict rules with their own children. Bill Gates, founder of Microsoft, ignored his children's pleas for phones and didn't allow them until they were fourteen. Steve Jobs' biographer Walter Isaacson wrote that "Every evening Steve made a point of having dinner at the big long table in their kitchen, discussing books and history and a variety of things." When Jobs introduced the iPad, he was asked how his own children liked it. He replied that they hadn't experienced it.[24] Many in the technology industry use the following guidelines with their own children:[25]

- No screens during the school week. As children get older and need a computer for schoolwork, the rule loosens. But a firm cut-off time is put in place.

- Limit screen use on weekends.

- No social media. (A tough one, especially for high schoolers. If you allow it, educate yourself about and monitor it.)

- No screens in bedrooms. They must be used in common spaces.

- No phones or devices at mealtimes.

These rules may seem draconian, but children whose parents enforce them are fortunate. In the classroom, it's easy to see which children live in households with few technology restrictions. One of the telltale signs is heightened distractibility. It's often very hard for children who spend a lot of time in front of screens to pay attention in class and stay focused on whatever the task at hand might be. Another telltale sign is lack of engagement, as passive entertainment can dull intellectual curiosity and agency. Patience with tasks that require attention to detail may be in short supply as well. Children who don't have a lot of tech distractions come to school better prepared for the sustained attention and deep concentration that learning requires.

## DON'T Expect a Magic Pill, but DO Look Forward to Positive Results

Reading from birth is not a panacea or formula for guaranteeing success in school or life. But what it will do is give your child that Invisible Toolbox of essential pre-literacy skills that every child needs in order to be successful. And it will forge a bond between you and your child that is critical for your child's well-being. Your positive attitude toward your child's learning and school has a huge impact on them.

I have encountered many students who struggled with reading during my long teaching career, many of whom received special services to support their learning in the classroom. Often these students were deemed "learning disabled," a vague and often-misunderstood term that refers to differences in the way the brain processes visual or auditory information. That there was actual neurological processing impairment may have been the case with some of these children, but just as often I observed that many of these students struggled because they were missing foundational pre-literacy skills or lacked emotional support outside of school.

I will never forget Jeremy, a third grader who clearly had a visual processing issue that made decoding words and reading aloud difficult. He struggled to decipher the words on a page and read aloud haltingly, but his comprehension was outstanding. One would never guess, listening to his labored oral reading, that he could understand what he read so well. But Jeremy had been read to all his life and was emotionally supported by his parents, so he had the internal infrastructure of reading in place and was highly motivated. These factors enabled him to persevere and achieve his potential despite his neurological processing challenges.

Some children, like Jeremy, actually do have genuinely organic learning disabilities, which means that they are born with brains that are wired differently. Many children who end up in special education, however, are there because they have missed out on critical pre-literacy development from very early on and suffer from a deficit of language skills. As we have seen, the emotional component of the parent-child bond is closely tied in with the development of language skills through speaking and reading, so when a child is lacking in language, it can also mean there is a weakened parent-child bond. These children suffer then, from both a deficit in language and a deficit in emotional support. School is a painful uphill struggle for them.

While reading from birth doesn't guarantee that a child will not be challenged in some way, it will build a foundation of skills and important emotional support that will prepare them for meeting the world of school to the very best of their ability.

# DON'T Believe It's Too Late to Begin Reading Aloud to Your Child

You may not have had the time or ability to read to your child when they were younger, and you may feel there is no way you can begin now that they are in school and don't even seem to enjoy reading. But it's not too late.

The key to inspiring an older child to read is to find out what interests them and support that. Is your child a horse lover or a soccer player? Do they love fashion or art? There are books—fiction and nonfiction—about nearly every subject imaginable. Visit your library together and ask the children's librarian for recommendations. Browse the bookstores together. Search for the subject in children's books on Amazon. Turn a read-aloud time into a nightly ritual that doesn't require your child to give up daytime activities they enjoy. When they're in bed and it's time for lights out, spend a few minutes reading aloud to them before saying goodnight. Your child won't protest, as this will not only allow more time to "stay up," but also doesn't require the sacrifice of anything they would rather be doing. Soon your child will come to expect this ritual and enjoy it.

I've often observed that children spark to activities that show their parent's interest in *them*. They want to connect with you.

## DO Help Your Child
## Build Their Own Personal Library

One of my favorite ideas for helping expectant parents build a library for their child begins with the baby shower. When guests are asked to bring a wrapped copy of their favorite book, the new baby is welcomed into the world with a personal library already in place.

Another favorite comes from advice columnist Amy Dickinson's "A Book on Every Bed" idea. Each year on her mother's birthday in early December, she steps away from readers' questions in her "Ask Amy" column to advocate for literacy. Dickinson attributes her passion for reading to her mother, with whom she shared a lifelong love for and conversation about books. For Christmas, or any holiday or birthday, she recommends placing a wrapped book on the foot of a child's bed, so that it's the first thing they wake up to on that special day. Once your child unwraps it, snuggling up and sharing it together makes a lasting memory.

When friends and relatives ask your advice about gifts for your child, don't hesitate to recommend books. They will be read and treasured long after a toy is played with and discarded. I was always impressed by a book-loving friend of mine with four daughters, who invariably sent her girls to birthday parties with gifts of gorgeous books of great quality, beautifully wrapped.

Explore options for free books. If your area participates in Dolly Parton's Imagination Library, you can register your child (from birth to age five) to receive an age-appropriate, high-quality book delivered free to your home every month. If you don't live in a participating region, you might consider getting the program started by becoming an area coordinator. Also, check out the newsletters and websites of children's authors and publishers, as many have sign-ups for free giveaways. You'll also be able to find out when your favorite author is coming to town and when book festivals and read-aloud events are happening.

## DO Visit Your Local Library and Get Your Child a Card of Their Own

Using the library encourages children to regularly and frequently make their own reading choices. When books are purchased, children have to make a greater commitment, which often necessitates adult involvement in the decision-making process. Unlike a bookstore or online shopping, browsing and sampling are not restrictive. The world of books is a child's oyster in a library.

Having a library card of one's own as a child is empowering because it implies both responsibility and privilege. Parents also should have and use their own cards. Making regular trips to the library in which both parent and child check out their own books—and shared books, too, for read-aloud time—communicates a powerful message to a child about the value, pleasure, and importance of reading.

I've seen the number of students who have library cards and use their local library dwindle in recent years. Many of them use only their school library or buy their books online. While both of these venues are also fine, they are missing out on the uniqueness of what their public library has to offer—limitless browsing, freedom of choice, and the frequent reminder of the value of reading that comes when they visit regularly with a parent and exercise this privilege with their very own library card.

## DO Find Creative Ways to Encourage Your Child to Read More, Independently

Common Sense Media recently reported that "US Children Read, But Not Well or Often."[26] According to this study, as children grow up, the amount of time spent reading for pleasure drops. With the myriad distractions of contemporary life, especially as children grow into adolescence, it's no wonder. When we help our young child experience their daily reading habit as a comforting space to come home to, there is a greater likelihood they will continue to find pleasure reading an oasis for themselves as they grow older and their lives become more complex.

A colleague of mine had a clever idea for encouraging his fourth-grade son to do more independent reading. He bought him a headlamp, the type used for cave-exploring, and granted him the privilege of using it after lights out. The novelty and cool factor of the headlamp, the dispensation to stay up later, and the gift of his first *Percy Jackson and the Olympians* novel turned the corner for this boy. He became an avid reader, and the following school year, his parents saw a striking improvement in his reading and vocabulary scores. The moral of this story is that a child needs to come to view reading as a value-added proposition. For children who feel that reading a book threatens to take the place of an activity they value more, finding that space in their day when it does not detract from another activity is the key. Bedtime is often that time.

One of the reasons it's so important to begin reading to a child regularly from early on is that an imprinting occurs and a habit is built. As a child grows and new pastimes come to be important—whether it's shooting hoops, building Legos, or simply completing homework—they will find a way to include it in their daily routine.

## DO Allow Discussions About What You Read Together to Emerge Naturally

As with any interaction with a child of any age, engaging together with the story is an endeavor that requires us as parents to be sensitive to the child in the moment. Forcing interaction, probing with questions, or expecting responses when a child is tired or overwhelmed is counterproductive and may evoke a negative response. Overeager parental engagement can result in a child shutting down to protect their inner world from contact that feels invasive. Being present to a child means that we cue into their feelings and mood and respond to them appropriately.

# DON'T Discourage Your Child from Reading Fluff, but DO Guide Them into Reading What Is Developmentally Appropriate

Children are drawn to books that they need to read. In the film *Shadowlands*, screenwriter William Nicholson wrote these words for C. S. Lewis: "We read to know we are not alone." I believe this is true for children as well as adults. The drive to connect is apparent even in their reading choices.

As I mentioned earlier, I was on a limited diet of Trixie Belden mysteries during my elementary school years. As an adult, I can now understand why. The blurb on the back covers of all the books in the series went like this: *"Would you like to—solve mysteries? belong to a secret club? ride, swim, travel, go to parties with the best friends in the world? Then the wonderful adventures of Trixie Belden are written just for you. Don't miss a single one!"* I didn't miss a single one, and I read and reread them many times over because the life Trixie lived was the life I aspired to for myself. I borrowed much from these books, bringing elements into my own world of play that included forming a secret club in my neighborhood with my best friend. We even had matching jackets with club patches that we sewed—just like Trixie. We pretended our bikes were horses, gave them names, and rode around the neighborhood on the lookout for suspicious behavior and mysteries to solve—just like Trixie. Trixie Belden mysteries were not great literature, but the world depicted was one that I needed emotionally and imaginatively at that time in my life. Because I loved reading, I eventually found my way to books of greater substance.

If we use the lens of emotional need to consider the popularity of books like *Diary of a Wimpy Kid*, it's not difficult to understand the attraction. Flawed hero Greg could be any child who struggles with self-doubt and feels a bit out of step. He writes about his life in a way that is both funny and relatable. Part of *Captain Underpants'* appeal is in addressing, also with humor, the forbidden—those subjects children quickly learn are taboo, but that they desperately want to talk about, or at least acknowledge. These books are entertaining, but also appeal to the reader's need for reassurance.

As you oversee the books your child selects, be open-minded, but don't be afraid to guide and set limits for them. Keep in mind the stage your child is in developmentally. Children whose independent reading ability outstrips their developmental age may need particular oversight. Outstanding readers in the older elementary grades often gravitate toward Young Adult (YA) books that are written for teenagers. While a YA book may be appropriate in terms of reading level, it may also deal with themes that are beyond a child's developmental ability to grasp. Introducing a child to issues they may not yet be emotionally equipped to deal with can be anxiety-producing. I run into this quite a lot with the ten- and eleven-year-olds I teach, and advise parents to not only be aware of their child's choices, but to read the books alongside them as well, so that they can be discussed together.

## DO Introduce Your Child to Quality Literature and the Classics

The classics are more challenging to read than many books children are naturally attracted to and, since they may not find them on their own, they are often a great choice for reading aloud. The vocabulary is more sophisticated and the themes are deeper, both of which afford an excellent opportunity for broadening your child's horizons emotionally and intellectually. Because they were written in another period of time, they provide a wonderful opportunity to discuss how life was different then. I've found that children need to be taken by the hand in order to discover the treasure in these books they might not otherwise be drawn to, *and* that they end up loving them. While children's classics do have cross-generational, universal appeal, the truth is they are best appreciated within a child's particular developmental window. I'll always regret that I didn't read *Anne of Green Gables* when I was eleven—Anne's age. I loved it as an adult, but still wonder how it might have affected me had I encountered it as a child.

# DO Keep in Mind that in Reading Aloud to Your Child You Are Sharing a Priceless Gift: Yourself

Creating a ritual of reading aloud with your child will grant them the gift of all the tools they will need in their Invisible Toolbox as they begin their journey to kindergarten and life beyond. Remember, too, that as you share books, you share an equally precious gift with your child—yourself. And they will always be grateful for it.

# Recommended Resources

*The Awakened Family: How to Raise Empowered, Resilient, and Conscious Children*, Shefali Tsabary, PhD (Penguin Books, 2017; 368 pages)

*100 Best Books for Children: A Parent's Guide for Making the Right Choices for Your Young Reader, Toddler to Preteen*, Anita Silvey (Houghton Mifflin, 2004; 192 pages)

*The Big Disconnect: Protecting Childhood & Family Relationships in the Digital Age*, Catherine Steiner-Adair and Teresa H. Barker (Harper, 2014; 384 page)

*1001 Children's Books You Must Read Before You Grow Up*, Julia Eccleshare (Universe, 2009; 960 pages)

*In Defense of Read-Aloud*, Steven Layne (Stenhouse Publishers, 2015; 200 pages)

*Magic Trees of the Mind: How to Nurture Your Child's Intelligence, Creativity, and Healthy Emotions from*

*Birth through Adolescence*, Marian Cleeves Diamond and Janet Hopson (Plume, 1999; 480 pages)

*The New York Times Parent's Guide to the Best Books for Children: 3rd Edition Revised and Updated*, Eden Ross Lipson (Harmony, 2000; 560 pages)

*The Read-Aloud Handbook, Seventh Edition*, Jim Trelease (Penguin Books, 2013; 384 pages)

*Reading Magic: Why Reading Aloud to Our Children Will Change Their Lives Forever*, Mem Fox (Mariner Books, 2008; 208 pages)

*Reading with Babies, Toddlers and Twos: A Guide to Laughing, Learning and Growing Together through Books*, Susan Straub and KJ Dell'Antonia (Sourcebooks, 2013; 304 pages)

*What Great Parents Do: 75 Simple Strategies for Raising Kids Who Thrive*, Erica Reischer (TarcherPerigee, 2016; 240 pages)

*The Whole-Brain Child: 12 Revolutionary Strategies to Nurture Your Child's Developing Mind*, Daniel J. Siegel and Tina Payne Bryson (Bantam, 2012; 192 pages)

# Recommended Reading Lists Per Age Group

With a seemingly infinite number of wonderful books in existence, how does one even begin to create a list when it cannot include all of them? It seemed a daunting problem. I knew what my favorites were, but that was hardly objective, nor was it all-inclusive. Then the answer came to me: *ask the experts.* The following recommendations come from those who have been reading aloud to children for a long time: teachers, librarians, parents, grandparents, and professionals in the publishing world. I present to you their top picks, a nice mix of classic and contemporary titles. Of course, I've thrown in a few of my own. Keep in mind, these are general, fluid categories regarding age and interest. Your toddler, for example, may very well enjoy books that I've included in the preschool/early-elementary section, and elementary-school-age children may still enjoy picture books. The important thing when choosing books to read aloud is to take your cues from your child.

## Baby/Toddler Books

*The Big Red Barn,* Margaret Wise Brown

*Brown Bear, Brown Bear, What Do You See?*
    Bill Martin, Jr.

*Clap Hands,* Helen Oxenbury

*The Foot Book,* Dr. Seuss

*From Head to Toe,* Eric Carle

*Goodnight, Gorilla,* Peggy Rathmann

*Goodnight Moon,* Margaret Wise Brown

*Hand, Hand, Fingers, Thumb,* Al Perkins

*I Kissed the Baby,* Mary Murphy

Little Blue Truck (series), Alice Schertle

*Mary Engelbreit's Mother Goose: One Hundred Best
    Loved Verses,* Mary Engelbreit

*"More More More," said the Baby,* Vera B. Williams

*Pat the Bunny (Touch and Feel Book),* Dorothy Kunhardt

*Peek-a-Who,* Nina Laden

*The Runaway Bunny,* Margaret Wise Brown

*We're Going on a Bear Hunt,* Michael Rosen

## Preschool/Early Elementary

*Are You My Mother?* P. D. Eastman

*The Big Orange Splot,* Daniel Pinkwater

The Boxcar Children (series), Gertrude Chandler Warner

*Busy, Busy World,* Richard Scarry

*The Cat in the Hat,* Dr. Seuss

*Chicka Chicka Boom Boom,* Bill Martin, Jr.

*Chickens Aren't the Only Ones,* Ruth Heller

*The Complete Tales of Peter Rabbit,* Beatrix Potter

Curious George (series), H. A. and Margret Rey

*The Day the Crayons Came Home,* Drew Daywalt

*Dinosaurumpus,* Tony Mitton

*Harold and the Purple Crayon,* Crockett Johnson

*Hershel and the Hanukkah Goblins,* Eric Kimmel

*How Rocket Learned to Read,* Tad Hills

*The House That Jack Built,* Jeanette Winter

*If You Give a Mouse a Cookie,* Laura Numeroff

*The Important Book,* Margaret Wise Brown

*The Little Engine That Could,* Watty Piper

*The Little Mouse, the Red Ripe Strawberry, and the Big Hungry Bear,* Don and Audrey Wood

Madeline (series), Ludwig Bemelmans

*Make Way for Ducklings,* Robert McCloskey

*Miss Rumphius,* Barbara Cooney

*Monster Mama,* Liz Rosenberg

My Father's Dragon (series), Ruth S. Gannett

*Olivia,* Ian Falconer

*The Polar Express,* Chris Van Allsburg

*Tikki Tikki Tembo,* Arlene Mosel

*Tinker and Tom and the Star Baby,* David McPhail

*This Is Not My Hat,* Jon Klassen

*The Velveteen Rabbit,* Margery Williams

*The Very Hungry Caterpillar*, Eric Carle

We Are in a Book! (An Elephant and Piggy Book) (series),
     Mo Willems

*Weslandia*, Paul Fleischman

*Where the Wild Things Are*, Maurice Sendak

*Yo! Yes?* Chris Raschka


## Elementary and Up

*The Adventures of Tom Sawyer*, Mark Twain

*Anne Frank, Diary of a Young Girl*, Anne Frank

Anne of Green Gables (series), L. M. Montgomery

Betsy-Tacy (series), Maud Hart Lovelace

*Black Beauty*, Anna Sewell

*A Bridge to Terabithia*, Katherine Paterson

*Caddie Woodlawn*, Carol Ryrie Brink

*Charlotte's Web*, E. B. White

*A Child's Garden of Verses*, Robert Louis Stevenson

The Chronicles of Narnia (series), C. S. Lewis

*The Count of Monte Cristo,* Alexandre Dumas

*D'aulaires' Book of Greek Myths,* Ingri d'Aulaire and
    Edgar Parin d'Aulaire

Encyclopedia Brown (series), Donald Sobol

*From the Mixed-Up Files of Mrs. Basil E. Frankweiler,*
    E. L. Konigsburg

The Great Brain (series), John D. Fitzgerald

*Grimm's Fairy Tales,* Jacob and Wilhelm Grimm

*Harriet the Spy,* Louise Fitzhugh

Harry Potter (series), J. K. Rowling

Hatchet (series), Gary Paulsen

*Holes,* Louis Sachar

*The Hundred Dresses,* Eleanor Estes

*Lassie Come Home,* Eric Knight

Little House on the Prairie (series), Laura Ingalls Wilder

*The Little Prince,* Antoine de Saint-Exupery

The Lord of the Rings (series), J. R. R. Tolkien

*Matilda,* Roald Dahl

*The Moffats,* Eleanor Estes

*Oliver Twist,* Charles Dickens

*Mrs. Piggle Wiggle,* Betty MacDonald

Percy Jackson and the Olympians (series), Rick Riordan

Ramona the Pest (series), Beverly Cleary

*Roll of Thunder, Hear My Cry,* Mildred D. Taylor

*The Secret Garden,* Frances Hodgson Burnett

A Series of Unfortunate Events (series), Lemony Snicket

*The Story of Ruby Bridges,* Robert Coles

*Stuart Little,* E. B. White

*The Tale of Despereaux,* Kate DiCamillo

*Tales of a Fourth Grade Nothing,* Judy Blume

*Winnie-the-Pooh,* A. A. Milne

*The Witches,* Roald Dahl

The Wonderful Wizard of Oz (series), L. Frank Baum

*Where the Red Fern Grows,* Wilson Rawls

*Where the Sidewalk Ends,* Shel Silverstein

*A Wrinkle in Time,* Madeleine L'Engle

# Recommended Websites and Organizations

American Association of Pediatricians' Recommendations for Children's Media Use:

www.aap.org/en-us/about-the-aap/aap-press-room/pages/american-academy-of-pediatrics-announces-new-recommendations-for-childrens-media-use.aspx

Born to Read, an American Library Association (ALA) program that partners with maternity hospitals and clinics to encourage parents to read from birth and tap into their library's resources from infancy onward. St. Louis County Library's expansive program, a model for the nation, has been adopted by every maternity hospital and clinic in the area.

www.slcl.org/content/born-read

Caldecott Medal and Honor Books from 1938 to the present, available at the ALA's website. This award is given each year to the artist of the most distinguished American picture book for children.

www.ala.org/alsc/awardsgrants/bookmedia/caldecottmedal/caldecottmedal

Dolly Parton's Imagination Library, a nonprofit organization that promotes early childhood literacy by giving free age-appropriate books to children from birth to age five.

www.imaginationlibrary.com

John Hopkins Center for Talented Youth's Recommended Reading Lists by grade level.

cty.jhu.edu/talent/after/index.html

Newbery Medal and Honor Books from 1922 to the present, available at the ALA's website. The Newbery Medal is awarded annually to the author of the most distinguished contribution to American literature for children.

www.ala.org/alsc/awardsgrants/bookmedia/newberymedal/newberymedal

Reach Out and Read, a nonprofit that gives young children a foundation for success by incorporating books into pediatric care and encouraging families to read aloud together.

www.reachoutandread.org

The Children's Reading Foundation, a national nonprofit with community-based reading foundation chapters and early childhood education programs across the country and in Canada. The foundation serves families, schools, and communities by providing proven programs, tools, and research to help nurture a child's development from birth through third grade in ways that foster essential early literacy, math, and social-emotional skills.

www.readingfoundation.org

The Invisible Toolbox, the author's website. Teaches that reading aloud to children from infancy enhances the parent-child bond that nurtures social-emotional well-being and builds the Toolbox of language skills necessary for success in school and life. Offers helpful information on diverse issues relating to literacy, education, and parenting.

theinvisibletoolbox.org

# Acknowledgments

This book was made possible through the indispensable work of Sarah Branham, Julia Lord, Brenda Knight, Robin Miller, and the entire Mango team. Emma Dryden, heartfelt thanks to you for setting the chain of connection with these remarkable talents in motion. Sandy Hughes, Jaime Payne, Sally Dailey, Peg Tichacek, and Sue Trantham Rector, your early support for the idea of *The Invisible Toolbox* encouraged me to take the next steps. The outstanding colleagues I've been privileged to teach with have made the world of school a dynamic place to work and learn. To the students I have encountered through all the years, thank you for teaching me as much as or more than I have taught you. Justin Rogers, you and your overflowing Toolbox continue to inspire me. I am deeply grateful to you all.

# About the Author

Kim Jocelyn Dickson (BS University of Missouri-Columbia; MA Princeton Theological Seminary) is a parent, educator, author, and lifelong lover of books. She has nearly thirty years of experience in the elementary school classroom, has taught in public and private schools in the East, Midwest, and West Coast of the United States, and currently teaches literature and writing at an independent school in Southern California. Kim is also the author of various articles on psychology, literature, biography, women's issues, and religion, as well as the book *Gifts from the Spirit: Reflections on the Diaries and Letters of Anne Morrow Lindbergh*, Crossroad, NY, 2002.

# Endnotes

[1] www.nationsreportcard.gov/reading/
nation/achievement/?grade=4

[2] www.aecf.org/m/resourcedoc/aecf-
EarlyWarningConfirmedExecSummary-2013.pdf

[3] balancedreading.com/Scholastic_reading_facts.pdf

[4] Touch is as Important to Infant Health as Eating and Sleeping.
www.drgreene.com/touch-is-as-important-to-infant-health-as-eating-
and-sleeping

[5] How to Keep Babies Calm, Happy, and Emotionally Healthy.
www.parentingscience.com/stress-in-babies.html

[6] Susan Brink. "Through a Newborn's Senses." Los Angeles Times,
May 11. 2013.

[7] Ibid.

[8] Ibid.

[9] Grace Bluerock. www.huffingtonpost.com/grace-bluerock/5-most-valuable-life-lessons-i-learned-hospice-worker_b_7499030.html

[10] Jim Trelease. The Read-Aloud Handbook, (New York: Penguin Books, 2006), p. 13.

[11] Ibid.

[12] Ibid., 16.

[13] Annie Murphy Paul. ("Your Brain on Fiction," New York Times, March 18, 2012)

[14] Ibid.

[15] Ibid.

[16] Ibid.

[17] www.psychologytoday.com/blog/the-athletes-way/201412/can-reading-fictional-story-make-you-more-empathetic

[18] "Social and Emotional Well-Being: The Foundation for School Readiness." WestED Center for Prevention and Early Intervention, California's Infant, Preschool, and Family Mental Health Initiative. www.wested.org/online_pubs/cpei/social-emotional.pdf. p. 7.

[19] Ibid. p. 9.

[20] Dr. James Loder. Developmental Psychology Lecture, Princeton Theological Seminary, Princeton, New Jersey.

[21] Literacy Development in Infants and Toddlers: Research Findings www.speechpathology.com/articles/lix-teracy-development-in-infants-and-1732

[22] www.nytimes.com/2014/10/12/us/is-e-reading-to-your-toddler-story-time-or-simply-screen-time.html

[23] www.bbc.com/news/health-30574260
E-books damage sleep, doctors warn

[24] www.independent.co.uk/life-style/gadgets-and-tech/news/bill-gates-children-no-mobile-phone-aged-14-microsoft-limit-technology-use-parenting-a7694526.html

[25] www.theguardian.com/technology/2015/may/23/screen-time-v-play-time-what-tech-leaders-wont-let-their-own-kids-do

[26] www.reuters.com/article/us-usa-reading-idUSKBN0DS04L20140512

Printed in the USA
CPSIA information can be obtained
at www.ICGtesting.com
JSHW012259060924
69456JS00003B/32

9 781642 502039